SUCCESS MADE SIMPLE

SUCCESS MADE SIMPLE

Using Uncomplicated Rules
and Making Smart Choices

Don Harrison

Compass Flower Press
Columbia, Missouri

Published by Compass Flower Press
Columbia, Missouri
www.compassflowerpress.com

Disclosure: Results from implementing examples made in this book will vary from individual to individual, store to store, and bank to bank. Scenarios are meant to be illustrations of ways to facilitate and create success.

Cover design, book layout, and editorial assistance by Yolanda Ciolli

Library of Congress Control Number: 2020910763

ISBN: 978–1–951960–03–2

Dedicated to Aimee with my thanks.

The Talking Frog

One spring day I was walking along the Auxvasse Creek on a farm I own in Callaway County, Missouri, hunting morel mushrooms. Suddenly I heard someone holler at me. I looked down and at the edge of the water was a frog.

The frog looked up at me and said, "If you kiss me, I'll turn into a beautiful young princess."

So I bent down, picked up the frog, and put it in my pocket. I started walking again and the frog spoke up and asked, "Hey mister, didn't you hear me? I said if you kiss me, I will turn into a beautiful young princess!"

I pulled the frog out of my pocket and looked at it, nodded my head, and said, "Yes I heard you, but I think at this stage in my life I would rather have a talking frog."

What's a talking frog story got to do with success?

You're not stuck in a pocket like this frog, with no choice in life. The concepts in these pages can help anybody at any age, but if you are a seventeen– or eighteen–year–old young adult graduating high school with questions about your future, this book may help you with some answers.

One of the most common questions asked is, "Should I attend college?" That really depends on what your personal goals are. I have had many friends who did not go to college and are very successful. I also have friends who entered college, but didn't finish, and friends who graduated from college, each with different levels of success. Many of these people still need help learning how to become successful.

College might not be for everyone. Factors to weigh can include economic hardship, lack of financial aid or scholarship offers, or just lack of interest in pursuing further formal education in an academic setting—all of which are completely understandable.

Your success is completely up to you. Your goals are set and obtained by you. Your attitude toward your success is what will drive you forward. The knowledge you gather, the work ethic you develop, being frugal and being smart about the things you do are choices that will determine your level of prosperity. Just a smile alone will take you a long way. People like to see a smile. You may not realize it, but even when you talk on the phone, the person on the other end of the line can tell when you are smiling!

This book is meant to help you be successful whether you go to college or not. Starting at a young age is even better. Some of the knowledge I will share I learned when I was only sixteen years old.

Introduction

Everyone wants to be successful. It's a simple, obvious fact of life.

We think to ourselves, "Why can't that be me?" Most people are inclined to live their lives thinking this way because they do not properly manage their money or time. They live paycheck to paycheck, buy lottery tickets every week hoping to win the big jackpot, and waste their money on petty, insignificant things. They are unaware of the unprecedented economic opportunities that surround them. These habits and lack of awareness are absolutely destructive to the financial goals we all strive for.

The path to success comes down to the philosophical choices that you make as an individual. You are the one who has to make the critical financial decisions for your life.

Unlike the thousands of other books on success, this book provides ordinary people with useful, realistic, simple concepts and objectives to create a financial structure built for success. It is not a get–rich–quick scheme. It requires time, discipline, patience, and determination to execute such a financial strategy. I hope these suggestions inspire you and provide you the insight to make the changes in your life that will help you overcome challenges on your path to success.

My Beginning

I think this all started for me when I was sixteen and got my first car. I'd only had it a few months when the brakes went out—and guess what? I had no money to fix them. I had been spending every dime I made just having fun like most every kid. I felt I had no choice but to go to my older brother and borrow some money. Boy, was that a lesson!

He preached to me and told me to save my money and not even buy a pack of chewing gum. At the time, I found it hard to listen to him preach to me about money, but I needed my brakes fixed. From that day forward I made sure that I saved some money. Maybe it was just so I didn't have to listen to another sermon.

Anyway, that was a good exercise in learning, and at sixteen years old, my brother had given me my first lesson for success! Thanks, Big Brother!

Success does not only mean money. It can mean different things to different people. Success is defined by what you want or wish for—the things that make you the happiest in your life. Your success can be built around financial independence, family, friends, etc. What you desire will determine your goals for success. Making lists of things you want in life will help you define your goals. You should save your lists and review them from time to time. Later when you look at them again, you will be surprised by how many things on the lists you have accomplished!

Lists tell your mind to be ready for opportunity and success, even when you are not thinking about it. A list is the beginning of defining goals.

The more time and effort you put into defining your goals and developing plans to accomplish them, the better you will get at reaching your aims and the more success you will have.

Most every successful person consistently invests time and effort into the goals they set for themselves. Most athletic ball players have some talent, but on top of that they work really hard to develop that talent to be the best!

I spent time coaching youth basketball a few years ago. I started with kids in the fourth grade. On one particular team, I had a player who had the burning desire and aptitude to be great. Sure enough, to this day he plays pro basketball overseas! He is a humble person who worked very hard to develop the gift he had. I think without that extra effort he would have been just an average ball player. He had a strong desire to succeed when he was in the fourth grade and still has it. I am proud of him and he should be proud of himself.

When he is not playing ball he is teaching basketball skills to kids. It is important to pass along what people teach you (kind of a payback for what people did for you), plus it leaves a good feeling in your heart. Sharing and being thankful is a way of showing appreciation for what your mentors have done for you.

Any basketball team, any football team—any successful team, sports or otherwise—puts in time, dedication, and practice. This is what makes them the best. Most have some natural talent, but the best put the most effort into their game. They make sure they are prepared for their game.

Reading this book will give you information you will need to get started on your journey to successfully reaching your goals in life. Gaining the knowledge itself is fairly easy. But it is entirely up to you to apply it.

The more you do something, the better you get at it. You must have the want or desire to be successful— not for one day, one week, or one year—but day after day, week after week, year after year. Success won't happen overnight. It takes time. Your consistent determination and effort will be the deciding factor in your amount of prosperity. The sooner you get started the better. If you never start, you will never achieve success.

As a kid being raised primarily by my mom, I was living in what most people would call poverty. My father had a real problem with alcohol and his social lifestyle. It was rough at times for my mom, but with some help from my uncles and aunts on my mom's side, we got by okay.

On my father's side of the family, they were all good people, but their priority was different. They lived a partying lifestyle, living from paycheck to paycheck.

My mom's side of the family seemed to be a little more successful. They had nicer vehicles and owned their homes.

By having two different kinds of families as models, I saw that I had a choice: my mom's family lifestyle, or my father's family lifestyle. It was an easy choice for me.

Many people don't ever see or know that there are different lifestyles other than the one they are living.

I was lucky; and I was thankful my uncles and aunts on my mom's side of the family became my mentors and helped my mom raise my brother and sister and me. I guess you could say that the people on my dad's side of the family were my mentors also, but they taught me things *not* to do. Don't misunderstand me, I loved my dad and his side of the family very much, just not their lifestyle!

The Importance of Mentors

A mentor is someone you look up to. You want as many as you can get. They are friends and more. All my uncles were mentors to me. They helped me through life and taught me many things, and I paid attention to them. I learned different things from each of them. My mentors included bosses, friends, and others. I was taught to always do my best at my jobs no matter what the pay.

Even now, I still have many mentors in my life. Some of them are very good friends. I have also been a mentor to several of them. Mentors learn from each other. I learn from them and they learn from me. I practice being a good listener to better learn from others.

I also try to pass along the things I learn. I have used this concept with my son and daughter, and I am proud of them for their accomplishments.

Try to be around people who are successful. They are the people in your life you will learn the most from.

The Drive for Success

Several things really drive me for success. One early and strong motivator was the fact that I was brought up in near–poverty conditions, and I would not wish that on anybody. I have no desire to ever go back to that lifestyle.

Another big incentive for me was a situation that occurred when I was in junior high school. I was on the school basketball team. Most of the players on the team started a club against me, calling me names. I finally quit the team, but the name–calling went on for a couple of years.

Finally, I had enough, and I got into a fight with one of them, and thank God, it ended all the bullying. Looking back, I almost could thank them. I found I could change my situation, which made me even more driven to success!

I think what defines you is how you handle challenges and rise above adversity. You can start with nothing and still be very successful!

Successful Habits

Most of us know what we want, but we lack the tools and practical understanding of how to get there. This book is written to give you examples and details that will help make you successful. I tried to use a simple format to make it easy for you to understand, and get you started on your way to prosperity.

Success requires work, but mostly it is about changing your habits and learning a different way to think. Dedication, desire, knowledge, and most of all, learning to be frugal is required. It is important that you work hard and make money, but even more important than what you earn, is learning to save and then doing it!

I have seen plenty of examples of people who make very good money, but live above their means and end up broke!

How to Start Saving

Being frugal means don't buy what you don't need or can't afford. Always do your best to save. When I first got out of high school, I was working with two older men who were brothers. I am sure they had seen worse times by far than I ever had in life. In their coffee thermoses they had only hot water—no coffee. That really made me think at the time.

My mother raised me, my twin sister, and my brother pretty much by herself and she had no choice but to be frugal. Even with a job that didn't pay very well, she managed to save. When she passed away she had over $300,000 in the bank and her small house was paid for—and all her life she had a job that paid below average wages.

I have frequently watched people, including my employees, spend ten to fifteen dollars every morning at a convenience store for things they could very easily do without, and then go back for lunch. It is a habit worth changing!

Money you could spend at a convenience store

Items Purchased	Cost
Soda or coffee	$2.00
Cigarettes	$5.00
Donut	$0.65
Chips	$2.69
Lottery ticket	$2.00
One–day Total	$12.34
Weekly (Five–Day) Total	$61.70
Yearly (Fifty–Week) Total	**$3,085.00**

All in all, there are many ways to waste your money, but also there are many ways to be frugal and save.

To be successful, your best option is to be economical and work to set aside some of your money. It is your choice, and one worth making.

If you are broke and living from paycheck to paycheck you must change something or it will stay the same. You will continue to scrape by from paycheck to paycheck.

The first thing you must do is make a list of everything you buy that isn't really planned—whether you use cash, a debit or credit card, pocket change— every penny, every day, every week. Total up what you have spent to see where your money is going. Then, go through your lists and start to figure out where you are wasting money and what you can cut back on and save.

Next list everything you and your family spend money on. List everything—the stuff you need or have an obligation to pay *and* the stuff you buy on a whim. This tells you where *all* your money is going. It also should show you where you are wasting money. Your common sense will identify what you should cut so you can save money.

Try shopping more economically—even for groceries—use a list; buy a sale item without overstocking and have something different than planned for a meal; be smart and frugal—you will be surprised!

Note: Overstocking on sale groceries can cost you money because you will be prone to wasting more. ***The only thing you can't overstock is your savings account!***

The Real Deal: Looking at Necessary and Other Expenses

Expenditure	Amount	Cut? Y / N
Rent or House payment	$_____	
Insurance: —Home or Renter's —Auto Insurance —Health or Life Insurance	$_____ $_____ $_____	
Electric Bill	$_____	
Water, gas, trash	$_____	
Phone Bill	$_____	
Cable TV / Internet	$_____	
Car Payment	$_____	
Car Maintenance & Repairs (oil changes, tires, etc.)	$_____	
Gas for Car	$_____	
Credit card payment	$_____	
Food / Groceries	$_____	
Beverages (on the go) (Coffee, soda, alcohol)	$_____	
Eating out / Movies / Bars	$_____	
Cigarettes	$_____	
Vacations & Trips	$_____	
TOTAL MONTHLY	$_____	

Now look at your full list. Are you spending more than you make? Are you building up credit card debt? Charging your lunches and impulse purchases to a credit card usually means you are spending more than you make.

Think about what items you use that affect the monthly costs on your list. This is the time to assess your wants versus needs. Check to find out if changing phone plans and such will benefit your success.

We all have needs and wants, and it's important to know the differences between the two to become more successful. You don't need the best of everything. Your review of these things will help you with planning and achieving the goals you set.

Needs Versus Wants

Need	Want:	Alternate choices:
Work day lunch	Eat out ($6–$10 per day)	Pack a lunch and save the money ($2–$5 per day)
Phone	Great smart phone with all the options	Reconditioned or used smart phone, practical flip phone
Phone plan	Big plan includes unlimited minutes, unlimited internet	Cheaper plan, trac-phone service that keeps you on budget
New jeans	Designer Jeans $50	Discount store Jeans $20
Home	Big house: more room than you need	Smaller house: more affordable, don't collect junk
Car	New stylish car with lots of options	Slightly used reliable vehicle, but just point-A to point-B style

A necessity is something we need in order to accomplish a task. There are usually many options as far as price and features for us to choose from to satisfy a need. A want is something bought in the moment without weighing the options and financial consequences. This often results in having more than needed, and the cost of the extra features may keep you from meeting your goals in a timely manner.

If you have reviewed your spending habits, you will probably have found that you sometimes let your wants take over and you've been spending more than needed by habit, or by choosing fancier things to fulfill the same needs.

You don't always have to have the top of the line to get the job done, and with a competitively priced equivalent that will perform just as well, you'll save money. Recognizing these differences will help you set your goals.

The difference between a rich person and a poor person is two cents. The poor person earns one dollar and spends one dollar. The rich person earns one dollar and spends ninety–eight cents and saves the other two pennies. Always spend less than you earn.

*He who buys what he does not
need steals from himself.*

—Swedish Proverb

Planning and Goal Setting

There is a proverb that says "If you don't know where you're going, any road will get you there." The same goes for your financial life. If you do not set goals and plan, you are at a huge disadvantage to achieving wealth and success—and most of all—happiness. You will probably get by, but is that good enough? Probably not. That is why you need to develop a plan to direct you on your course. There will be bumps along the way, but if you continue to follow your plan you will find your way to your destination. I can't guarantee that you will become a financial icon, but I can guarantee that you have the potential to reach your financial goals.

An important step to achieving success is setting short– and long–term goals and devising a plan to reach them.

Your goals should be challenging, yet realistic and attainable. They should be specific and easily measurable. You should develop several short–term goals that ultimately lead into one or two long–term goals. You should also give yourself a time frame to reach certain goals. After all, most people are proven to work better under pressure. However, you should remain patient. You will not reach success overnight.

To implement your goals into a financial strategy, you have to review your current financial status, decide what financial feats you wish to conquer, and finally, devise a plan to accomplish them.

The Personal Net Worth Statement

One good way to start your planning is to complete a net worth statement. This will give you an overview of your current financial status and it will eventually provide you a reference point for evaluating your progress.

You should start by listing the full values of the things that you own (even if they are not paid off). These are assets. Assets include cash (under the mattress and in savings), your home, your vehicle, investments, and other things of worth. Include the total amount they are worth; you will be showing how much you still owe in your liabilities, so the math will work out.

After totaling your assets you should now list your liabilities.

A liability is money that is owed to creditors—banks and money lenders. Liabilities include mortgage balances owed, vehicle loan balances, student loan balances, credit card balances, and any other debts that remain unpaid.

When you have finished listing and totaling your liabilities, you should subtract that amount from the total of your assets. This is your net worth. If it is a positive number, your net worth is positive. You are already on your way to success! If the number is negative, do not be discouraged. After all, that is why I wrote this book! To help you climb your way to the top of the financial ladder, rung by rung.

Your net worth boils down to this simple fact: The total value of your assets minus the total dollar amount of your liabilities equals your net worth.

You can search online for an official Personal Net Worth Statement form like the banks use, but you'll find they have far more areas of assets and liabilities to list than you may have, so don't worry about all of that until you have such complications.

Keep it simple while you can. You know what you have, and can estimate or look up values and loan balances to make your list of assets and liabilities.

It might look like this:

Calculate Your Personal Net Worth

Item	Full Value *Asset*	Amount Owed *Liability*	Difference *Net Worth*
Vehicle	$10, 000	$6,200	$3,800
Cash on hand and in bank	$1,200	$0.00	$1,200
Credit Card	$0.00	$3,100	($3,100)
Totals	$11,200	$9,300	$1,900

In the scenario shown, the credit card balance is troublesome. It might mean you are spending more than you make, or you are accumulating unnecessary debt, but you can choose to change your habits and be frugal. With discipline and by carefully staying within your means you will be able to use a credit card, track your budgeted amount for its use, and pay the balance off each month—and still save money.

Form your Road Map to Success

Now that you know your daily money situation and where you are with your total finances—owned and owed, you have to map out where you want to be and a plan to get there. The program you outline will provide you a path to follow and a way to reassure yourself by tracking and evaluating your progress. This plan is like a road map for your journey, in this case, to success. Your plan will help you efficiently carry out your intentions to ultimately reach your goals and maximize your success. It is a declaration of what you can do and need to do in order to achieve financial security. You must be disciplined to not drift from the path. The key is to control your money. . . do not let it control you.

Factors for Goals and planning:

Most people spend more time planning their vacation than they spend planning their life! Successful people have goals and plans. They don't waste valuable time. As stated previously, success begins with goals and planning. In order to plan and set goals for yourself you need to educate yourself by reading more books and articles about strategies for saving money and ways to become successful.

Assessing how you spend your time is also very helpful in both setting and reaching your goals. It will speed up your success to begin to change some habits if you find you are overindulging in time wasting and/or money wasting activities.

Time Is Money
Working smarter and harder:
Look for time eaters.

Time Wasters	Money Waster	Productive Alternates
Internet: Gaming, cruising the net, impulse shopping	Spending money on unnecessary things	Research tutorials for new skills, related skills.
Too much TV	Drinking too much	Read more how–to and success books. Keep up on current events that may expose opportunities on the horizon.
Grocery shopping without a list	Spending more than your budget	Plan your list and stick to it when you shop.
Driving to the store to buy prepared food	Eating out too much	Learn to cook simple meals on a budget

A few years ago, I was working on a home I was building to sell. A little boy from the neighborhood who looked to be about twelve years old walked into the home while I was working. He asked me for an empty soda bottle he saw in the house. At that time there was a deposit on bottles, so if you returned the bottle for recycling you would receive money for it.

I asked the boy what he would do with the money if I gave him the bottle and he recycled it?

The boy said, "You know, most people are tight wads, but me, I'm what they call a loose wad." At twelve years old this kid was already on the wrong track for success.

Managing money properly and being frugal is very important to becoming successful. Now, there is such a thing as being too cheap. All you want is to be smart with the way you spend and save your money. Also, how you use your time is really important.

I once had a good friend tell me that if I didn't make enough money that I needed to start working one hour earlier each day.

So I did the math: If you made $15 an hour and could get the extra hours from your employer, or if you could bill out an extra $15 a day working for yourself by adding an hour to your work day, five days a week for 50 weeks a year comes to $3,750 a year, and in 20 years you'd have the opportunity to have $75,000 in the bank.

I have always tried to spend most of my time being productive. Even with my time outside my real job. I try not to waste too much time watching television or chatting on the phone. It's smart to limit time spent on these kinds of things. Remember, the more time and effort you put into your success, the more successful you will become.

Try to enjoy the simple things in life. Sometimes they are priceless. Just a walk in the woods or in a park can make for a great time that is rejuvenating— and smile always. Enjoy your time.

Examination of all your habits and spending should have prepared you for your own goal planning. You'll find that not all your goals will be about money. It's good to have goals that help you improve your habits.

Goals and Planning

ST stands for short–term goal
LT stands for long–term goal

Goal	Plan	Deadline
Get ahead Save money **ST & LT**	Work harder and smarter to not waste time or money	This is a lifetime commitment if you plan to get ahead
Buy a home **LT**	You should plan to have a 20% down–payment on a home, so you need to decide the price of home you want, and save your down payment.	Depending on your desired price, 5–7 years of saving and planning is probably realistic.
Better Car **ST**	Since new cars lose value as soon as you purchase them, used cars are often your best choice. Usually if you pick a car that is only two years old or newer with low mileage, you get more bang for your buck.	This goal can generally be obtained in twelve months.

Once you start making lists of your goals, you will find these lists expanding to include habits you feel you can change, and what they will mean to your success track. It's usually hard at first, but when you see your bank account grow, or get your first goal accomplished, you'll become more inspired to stay on track for yourself and for your employer. As I said before, I always did the best job I could no matter what the pay was. Your habits will be much better and you will feel great about your achievements. It won't be hard to smile and look at the good you are doing in your life for yourself and others.

Here's a scenario for buying a $200,000 home . . . .

Home Loan Options: Amortization
$200,000 Cost $40,000 Down Payment
$160,000 Loan at 6% Interest

Term	Monthly Payment	Total $ per Year	Total $ over term of loan
15 year	$1,350	$16,200	$243,000
20 year	$1,146	$13,752	$275,040
30 year	$ 959	$11,508	$345,240

On top of the bank payments shown, note that the average down payment to get financing is 20%, or $40,000 you must have saved to get a $200,000 house. Then you will also be paying real estate taxes and homeowners insurance, adding to your monthly payments.

You can see from these figures that there is a great advantage in financing your home over a shorter amount of time.

If you finance your home over 15 years versus 30 years, the cost savings is over $100,000. This $100,000 would have been interest the bank made from your loan. If you end up taking out a 30 year loan and can pay an extra $400 a month, all the extra money you pay is actually going toward the balance you borrowed (the principal), not interest, so you will be able to save that $100,000 —or even more, if you pay additional extra principal, and become closer to owning your home outright.

Always remember: the longer the term of finance, the more interest money you are giving to the bank on any kind of loan.

When Times Get Tough

The steps to success and prosperity outlined in this book will carry you far in your life. You will find that you have learned how to get out of almost any mess that comes your way—even messes you were not responsible for creating that extend beyond your personal life and finances. With the knowledge you gain from this book, you should always have a feeling of security.

When you know how to make money, and most of all, how to save and manage it by practicing these simple rules—and not live from paycheck to paycheck—you'll learn to save your money. Then, you'll always be ahead of the person who just wasted their money on unnecessary things.

No matter how well you live your life, you will still have some difficult times—that is part of life. The thing that is most important is how you handle those times. It's bound to happen sometime that the whole world seems to turn upside–down. This is the time to take up the practice of writing down your ideas. You don't want to forget a good idea that could benefit your success, and help others, too.

And don't forget that your attitude is your own. You can choose to get depressed and down in the dumps, but that's not going to make you feel any better. Finding out your bank account just got hit by a stock market slump is a time to look for different ways to put your money to work, and to see where you can use frugality in a new way to bring your numbers *and* your spirits up.

Let's say you lose your job, and you feel like there is nothing you can do. Remember—*you have choices*. Start an action list. Stay in touch with people as best as you can and find out if they have any ideas or know of a job position opening up that might be right for you. Brainstorming is actually great practice in problem–solving.

Here's another old saying, and it's true. "In every adversity there is opportunity."

If you have some extra money saved and things go south, I have found that often these difficulties can create more opportunity. When I've seen a circumstance that looks like it has potential money–making opportunity,

I've taken time to think through and weigh the possibilities of what might happen. On various occasions I have used my savings and made some good investments from buying during a decline in the economy. This kind of opportunity could come up for you. You don't always have to have huge amounts of money in the bank to profit from an obvious opportunity.

Because I have developed good habits of being frugal and saving money, I've been able to make some profitable investments on land and the stock market. It's not where you came from, it is where you want to go!

When I think about the stock market, I'd rather buy when prices are low, not when prices are high. Everything that goes up must come down.

I have always bought land and resold it. I've been able to make money when I've bought property at a good low price and sold it later when prices went up. It's probably not a good idea to just buy something with the hope that the price will go up. I think you can make money when you see a trend that selling prices are rising and you are able to buy at a good price; then sell when the right time comes.

I am always serious about the way I plan and live my life. I try not to be wasteful, and remember to be thankful for the things I have.

One secret to success in life is for a man to be ready for his opportunity when it comes.

—Benjamin Disraeli

Some of My Paths to Success

Just like most kids at the age of eighteen and fresh out of high school, I had no clue where I was going, much less what I was going to do with my life. So, I took a job working in construction and it seemed to be a decent job for me. The job paid what I thought was good money at the time. I lived at home with my mom, so I had very few bills other than a car payment and insurance for my car. Thanks to my mom I had the opportunity to save almost all my paycheck each week.

In about a year I had a little bit of money saved up, so I went in with my dad and we bought a six–acre tract of land for $2,400. We had a small pond built on it that cost about $600 and we also spent some time cleaning the place up.

There happened to be a mobile home on the place that was good enough to live in. My dad and one of his brothers moved into the trailer, and the next thing I knew they had caught it on fire. I made the decision to go solo on my investing.

We sold the place soon after that for $6,000. I took my part, $3,000 and with that money I set out to buy a forty–acre tract of land. The price was $6,000. I only had $3,000 so I had to borrow $3,000 from the bank. The banker told me that the land was not worth it, but I had half the money, so he loaned me the other $3,000. I sold it for $25,000.

I took the money and started my own construction business doing commercial masonry work and building houses.

As my business grew, I needed work trucks, so I went into business with a good friend rebuilding wrecked cars and trucks. I think of that friend as one of the smartest and most talented people I know.

I would buy wrecked trucks that only had a few thousand miles on them. At that time, they would cost around $5,000 to $6,000. After fixing them up I would have around $10,000 in a truck worth about $20,000–$25,000.

They were fully paid for, so I would go to the bank and borrow $20,000 against the truck. Then I would take the $20,000 and put into a CD (Certificate of Deposit). CDs earn interest on a timed interval—both the rate and time you have to leave the CD in the bank are set when you buy it.

Then I would make payments for three years. The $20,000 CD was savings in the bank, plus it was making interest money for me.

At the end of the three years the loan on the truck was paid off, so I would sell the truck for around $10,000 and take that money and buy another wrecked truck and fix it up and start all over again by borrowing another $20,000.

I had several trucks at a time. Doing that turnaround with five trucks enabled me to put $100,000 in savings and the work trucks I needed were costing me considerably less than new ones. Just something to think about.

Some people might look at this formula for borrowing to save as faulty thinking and a poor investment, but I felt it was a way to force myself to save. I was making good money and didn't want to fall into bad habits and spend it all, so this idea was worth it to me. I wasn't going to default on a truck loan, and I wasn't going to withdraw the CD before it matured and have to pay a penalty. Some of the years, the interest earned on CDs was really high. Plus I knew it couldn't hurt my relationship with the banker to have more funds in his bank, and it helped me build my net worth more quickly.

Some years later I decided a car wash would probably be a good money maker. I found a piece of land that was well suited for the purpose, and the woman who owned it offered to finance it for me. That was a good thing, and helped me get started. I built the car wash and it did very well from the first day it opened.

My kids were starting to drive, so I had them help me run the car wash and it gave them a job while they were in high school. It all worked out well. They had a little spending money, and I got a little work out of them. Since the first car wash was very successful, I built another one. After running them for five or six years I was offered a very good price for them both, so I sold them.

At that time our county was changing quickly, and not in a good way. The county's personal property and real estate taxes were continually increasing. The rules for building were getting more restrictive and the price for permits was getting higher. So, I took the money I got from selling the car washes and went six miles down the interstate to a different county. The taxes were cheaper, and there were no building permits or rules.

I also bought another tract of land and started a small industrial park. I built a new office building there, sold my old office building, and moved almost everything to the other county.

In 2008, when the economy crashed and put many people in a financial bind, I ended up buying a roll–off trash business for a very good price—about thirty cents on the dollar. I ran it for four or five years and sold it for a good profit.

Even when things seem tough, there can still be opportunities out there. Right now there are good deals out there, and people are selling land with owner financing. You just have to do some research and ask.

Looking for different types of opportunities is a way of life for me. For example, now I have a new truck and it is almost paid for, so I'm thinking about borrowing money against it and putting the loan money into a CD. Then I'll make payments again—just to keep up the habit of saving.

Two of the most expensive things in life are your home and your automobile. So, if you can build your house or save money on a used auto, you are way ahead of the people that must just go out and buy a house or buy a new car.

These are just some of the examples of things I have done and how I think. This is me.

When I first started working construction, I was on a job site and I was picking up nails someone had dropped on the ground. My boss told me not to pick them up because he was paying me more than what the nails were worth.

Always be smart about what you are doing and how you are thinking. Always have your best interests in mind.

It was good to learn the way my boss was thinking. Later when I started my own business, I realized just how much it cost my old bosses to give us fifteen minute breaks. There were taxes they paid into our Social Security, and Unemployment taxes, Workers' Comp insurance and expenses like that. It costs quite a bit more to have employees than just the paychecks.

When a $15 hourly worker was ten minutes late coming to work and didn't stay late or skip part of lunch break to make up the time, it cost the boss $2.50 each time. If this was a daily occurrence that's $12.50 a week, and almost an hour of lost time every week. So ten minutes a day, five days a week, fifty weeks a year cost the boss $625 a year and over forty hours. A guy would probably never get a raise and might even get fired if it became a bad habit.

Good habits will take you a long way with others, and with building your financial picture. You can start out slowly and learn how to save, and then build up a little at a time.

I had a healthy desire for success and always will. I also want others to be successful. I was working in a new subdivision the other day, and told the person I was working with that I was pleased to see the builders of today doing the same things to be successful as I did forty–six years ago, and it is still working for them. I am happy for them—I like being around people who are successful.

I have always thought that it's better to teach someone how to fish, not just give them the fish. There is more pride and satisfaction gained from catching fish than there is in just being given a fish. Pass the information you learn on to others: your family, friends and those around you. Remember that the examples you set and the habits you show affect your family and others.

The story I told you about the frog was just to loosen you up some. I want you to be serious about life, but also be able to take a break from it. Laugh, smile and enjoy your life. I told you about my childhood and some of my hard times just to give you the understanding that you can rise above hardships and be very successful.

Remember

Always be a fighter—never quit.

Always be ready with a smile and laugh.

Life can be very good.

My hope is that this book will help you.

Perseverance is not a long race; it is many short races one after the other.

—Walter Elliot

Last Thought

The price of a good book is about the same as one or two trips to a convenience store. Think about it! There are countless good books available that contain helpful information for you to learn good success tips from.

About the Author

Don Harrison has lived in Central Missouri his entire life, and while he may not have enjoyed every minute of it, he has always maintained a great sense of humor. That is probably one of his greatest assets.

His goal with this book is to help people determine a viable and satisfying path to success.

www.ingramcontent.com/pod-product-compliance
Lightning Source LLC
Chambersburg PA
CBHW022039090426
42741CB00007B/1134